Easy Peasy Russian!

Your Russian Phrase Book To Go!

by

Alina Volkov

Table of Contents

History and Introduction

The Russian language is one of the most commonly spoken languages in the world. This beautiful Slavic language is presently utilized by more than 164 million global inhabitants. Similar to other related Slavic languages, the Russian language originated from the Old Church Slavonic, which is a primordial language that was the basis for numerous contemporary Slavic languages.

Moreover, the Russian language belongs to the Indo-European group of languages that originated from the eastern subdivision of Slavic dialects that are diffused in Eastern Europe. One of the foremost characteristics of Russian one can highpoint is the utilization of its own alphabet (Cyrillic writing system) which is different from the Latin ABC employed in Western Indo-European groups of languages and utilizes 33 letters.

Thus, the Russian language appeared on the roots of east-Slavic dialects when Russian government institutions decided to cultivate a typical dialect comprehensible for the all ethnic groups in a similar way. Such a vernacular was grounded on the language of Polanians, the inhabitants of Kiev, the capital of Kievan Russia.

Therefore, this vernacular was the base of Old Russian historical language. The authentic alphabet developed in Russian territories first after the implementation of Christianity. The Cyrillic writing system was created in the IX century by brothers Methodius and Cyril. With the assistance of that writing system Greek religious paper works were decoded into Slavonic dialects.

Subsequently, the Cyrillic alphabet has diffused across the Slavic community and after the Kievan Russia's baptism, it became widely popular among the Eastern Slavic inhabitants. Moreover, the language was reformed and improved only in the XVIII century. In 1917-1918 it attained the contemporary Russian alphabet. The newest transformation of the language was performed in the beginning of the 1970s.

Pronunciation and Grammar

In comparison with English pronunciation, which habitually has more exclusions than regulations, Russian regulations of pronunciation are objectively understandable and unswerving. The Russian language can be called a phonetic language, which signifies that in general one Russian alphabetic character can be related to only one sound.

As an illustration, the letter "**K**" each and every time is uttered like "**k**", and the letter "**M**" each and every time is uttered like "**m**". In this way, Russian pronunciation is dissimilar to English pronunciation, where one alphabetic character can be pronounced in diverse ways according to a place where it is situated in a word. For example, there exists two dissimilar articulations for the letter "**c**" in such words as "captain" and "space". Hence, such dissimilarity practically never occurs in Russian language.

Therefore, Russian is a supple language that offers six cases of declension for each singular and plural adjective and noun, consequently this language doesn't require articles for indications. In Russian, there are three genders (neutral, feminine, and masculine) and verbs are presented in a perfect and imperfect phase in addition to the conjugation utilizing the three linguistic moods and three tenses.

Russian language correspondingly has numerous palatalized and sibilant consonant sounds in its pronunciation system, which is regulated by several unassuming pronunciation rules. One can likewise note the standard order of words in the sentence, according to which the subject is placed at the beginning of the sentence; the verb is situated intermediately and the object is always at the end of the clause.

Nevertheless, this sentence order is flexible in accordance with the framework of the discussion. Word construction habitually utilizes the source system of several big accustomed words originating from a single root with the supplement of a sequence of prefixes and suffixes.

Vowels

Latin / Cyrillic		English Sound
a / a		as "**ah**" in "Ah!" when it is stressed and as "**u**" in "cup" when it is unstressed
ye / e		as "**ye**" in "yellow" when it is stressed and as "**i**" in "picture" when it is unstressed
yo / ё		as "**yo**" in "yonder"
ee / и		as "**ee**" in "tweet" when it is stressed and as "**i**" in "pick" when it is unstressed
o / o		as "**o**" in "on" when it is stressed and as "**u**" in "sum" when it is unstressed
oo / у		as "**oo**" in "mood" when it is stressed and as "**u**" in "pull" when it is unstressed
no equivalent / ы		in order to pronounce the Russian sound "ы", you need to locate your tongue in the middle position between English sounds "**i**" in "pit" and "**u**" in "put".
eh / э		as "**e**" in "net"
yoo / ю		as "**u**" in "uniform"
ya / я		as "**ya**" in "yard"

Consonants

Latin / Cyrillic		English Sound
b / б		as "**b**" in "but" and as "**b**" in "bee" if followed by the soft sign or the "soft" vowels
v / в		as "**v**" in "voice and as "**v**" in "view" if followed by the soft sign or the "soft" vowels
g / г		as "**g**" in "go" and as "**g**" in "girl" if followed by the soft sign or the "soft" vowels
d / д		as "**d**" in "dial"
zh / ж		as "**s**" in "leisure"
z / з		as "**z**" in "zoom" and as "**z**" in "zeal" if followed by the soft sign or the "soft" vowels
k / к		as "**ck**" in "clock" and as "**k**" in "okay" if followed by the soft sign or the "soft" vowels
l / л		as "**l**" in "lump" and as "**l**" in "leak" if followed by the soft sign or the "soft" vowels
m / м		as "**m**" in "monk" and as "**m**" in "muse" if followed by the soft sign or the "soft" vowels
n / н		as "**n**" in "noon" and as "**n**" in "need" if followed by the soft sign or the "soft"

		vowels
p / п		as "**p**" in "pot" and as "**p**" in "pew" if followed by the soft sign or the "soft" vowels
r / p		as "**r**" in "run" but it is rolled
s / c		as "**s**" in "soup" and as "**s**" in "seed" if followed by the soft sign or the "soft" vowels
t / т		as "**t**" in "ten" and as "**t**" in "stew" if followed by the soft sign or the "soft" vowels
f / ф		as "**f**" in "fault" and as "**f**" in "few" if followed by the soft sign or the "soft" vowels
h / x		as "**h**" in "host" and as "**h**" in "huge" if followed by the soft sign or the "soft" vowels
ts / ц		as "**ts**" in "what's up"
ch / ч		as "**ch**" in "church"
sh / ш		as "**sh**" in "shake"
shch / щ		there is no full equivalent of "щ" in English, but it can be pronounced by combining "**sh**" and "**ch**"
j / й		as "**y**" in "may"
no equivalent /		"Hard sign" is rarely utilized as it points out a pause between the sounds

8

Ъ		
no equivalent / ь		"Soft sign" indicates the softness of the previous sound

Digraphs

Latin / Cyrillic		English Sound
dzh / дж		as "j" in "John"
zhzh / жж		no equivalent in English, this sound is pronounced similar to "g" in "gesture"
zhch / жч		no equivalent in English, this sound is pronounced similar to the "shch" or "щ"
zzh / зж		no equivalent in English, this sound is pronounced similar to "g" in "gender"

Diphthongs

Latin / Cyrillic		English Sound
ee / и:		as "ee" in "see"
ay / эй		as "ay" in "day"
ai / ай		as "i" in "time"
oi / ой		as "oy" in "toy"
ey / ей		as "ey" in "obey"
ooy / уй		no equivalent: the combination of "oo" as in "mood" and "y" as in "toy"
iy / ий		no equivalent: the combination of "i" as in "pick" and "y" as in "toy"

Everyday Phrases

	Translation (Latin / Cyrillic)	How to say it
Hello.	Zdravstvuyte / Здравствуйте	Zdrah-stvuy-tye
Good morning.	Dobroye utro / Доброе утро	Doh-broh-ye oot-roh
Good day.	Dobriy den / Добрый День	Doh-briy dyen
Good evening.	Dobriy vecher / Добрый вечер	Doh-briy veh-cher
Good night.	Spokoynoy nochi / Спокойной ночи	Spo-koy-noy no-chee
Hi.	Privet / Привет	Pree-vyet
Goodbye.	Poka / Пока	Po-kah
Nice to meet you.	Priyatno poznakomitsya / Приятно познакомиться	Pree-yah-tno poh-znah-ko-mee-tsah
How are you?	Kak dela? / Как дела?	Kahk deh-lah?
Fine, thank you.	Spasibo, horosho / Спасибо, хорошо	Spah-see-boh, hah-roh-shoh
What is your name?	Kak vas zovut? / Как вас зовут?	Kak vahs zoh-voot?
My name is.	Menya zovut / Меня зовут	Mye-nya zoh-voot

Yes.	Da / Да	Dah
No.	Net / Нет	Nyet
Please.	Pozhaluysta / Пожалуйста	Pah-zhah-luy-stah
Thank you.	Spasibo / Спасибо	Spah-see-boh
You are welcome.	Ne za shto / Не за что	Nye zah shtoh
Please, can you help me?	Ne mogli bi vi mne pomoch, pozhaluysta? / Не могли бы вы мне помочь, пожалуйста?	Nye moh-glee bee vee poh-mohch mnye, pah-zhah-luy-stah?
Excuse me.	Izvinite / Извините	Eez-vee-nee-tye
Pardon me.	Proshu proshcheniya / Прошу прощения	Proh-shoo proh-shchye-nee-ya
I am sorry	Prostite / Простите	Proh-stee-tye
Do you speak English?	Vi govorite po angliyski? / Вы говорите по английски?	Vee goh-voh-ree-tye poh un-gleey-skee?
Is there someone here who speaks English?	Tut kto-nibud govorit po angliyski? / Тут кто-нибудь говорит по английски?	Toot ktoh nee-bood goh-vog-reet poh un-gleey-skee?
Please repeat that!	Povtorite pozhaluysta / Повторите, пожалуйста	Poh-vtoh-ree-tye pah-zhah-luy-stah

I understand.	Ya ponimayu / Я понимаю	Yah poh-nee-mah-ju
I do not understand.	Ya ne ponimayu / Я не понимаю	Yah nye poh-nee-mah-ju
What does it mean?	Shto eto znachit? / Что это значит?	Shtoh etoh znah-cheet?
What time is it?	Kotoriy chas? / Который час?	Koh-toh-reey chahs?
Where is the bathroom?	Gde nahoditsya tualet? / Где находится туалет?	Gdye nah-ho-dee-tsah too-ah-let?
Where can I find a telephone?	Gde ya mogu nayti telefon? / Где я могу найти телефон?	Gdye yah moh-goo nay-tee teh-leh-fon?

Accommodation

	Translation (Latin / Cyrillic)	How to say it
Do you have any rooms available?	U vas est svobodniye nomera? / У вас есть свободные номера?	Oo vahs yest svoh-boh-dnee-yeh noh-meh-rah?
How much is a room for one person?	Skolko stoit nomer dlya odnovo cheloveka? / Сколько стоит номер для одного человека?	Skoh-lkoh stoh-eet noh-mehr dlya ohd-nhoh-voh che-loh-ve-kah?
How much is a room for two people?	Skolko stoit nomer dlya dvuh chelovek? / Сколько стоит номер для двух человек?	Skoh-lkoh stoh-eet noh-mehr dlya dvooh che-loh-vehk?
May I see the room first?	Mogu ya snachala uvidyet nomer? / Могу я сначала увидеть номер?	Moh-goo ya snah-cha-lah oo-vee-dyet noh-mehr?
Does the room come with...	V nomere est... / В номере есть...	V noh-mye-reh yest...
... a bathroom?	... vannaya komnata? / ... ванная комната?	... van-nah-yah kom-nah-tah?
... a telephone?	... telefon? / ... телефон?	... tye-leh-fon?
... bedsheets?	... postelnoye belye? / ... постельное бельё?	... poh-stel-noh-ye byel-yo?

… pillows?	… podushki? / … подушки?	… poh-doosh-kee?
… towels?	… polotentsa? / … полотенца?	… poh-loh-tyen-tsah?
… shower?	… dush? / … душ?	… doosh?
… a TV?	… televisor? / … телевизор?	… tye-lye-vee-zohr?
Do you have anything...	U vas est shto-nibud... / У вас есть что-нибудь...	Oo vahs yest shtoh-nee-bood...
… bigger?	… pobolshe? / … побольше?	… poh-bol-sheh?
… cleaner?	… pochishche? / … почище?	… poh-chee-shcheh?
… smaller?	… pomenshe? / … поменьше?	… poh-men-sheh?
… cheaper?	… deshevle? / … дешевле?	… dye-shev-leh?
… quieter?	… boleye tihoe? / … более тихое?	… boh-leh-ye tee-hoh-ye?
… better?	… poluchshe? / … получше?	… poh-looch-sheh
Do you offer...	U vas est... / У вас есть...	Oo vahs yest...
… a safe?	… seif? / … сейф?	… seif?
… lockers?	… zamki? / … замки?	… zam-kee?
Is breakfast included?	Zavtrak vkluchen? / Завтрак включен?	Zav-trahk vklyu-chyon?

Is supper included?	Uzhin vkluchen? / Ужин включен?	Oo-zheen vklyu-chyon?
When is breakfast?	Vo skolko zavtrak? / Во сколько завтрак?	Voh skoh-lkoh zav-trahk?
When is supper?	Vo skolko uzhin? / Во сколько ужин?	Voh skoh-lkoh oo-zheen?
Ok, I will take it.	Horosho, ya beru evo / Хорошо, я беру его	Hah-roh-shoh, yah bye-roo ye-voh
I will stay for... night(s).	Ya ostanus na... noch (nochey) / Я останусь на... ночь (ночей)	Yah os-tah-noos nah... nohch (noh-chey)
Can you suggest other hotels?	Vi mozhete posovetovat drugie oteli? / Вы можете посоветовать другие отели?	Vee moh-zheh-tye poh-so-vye-toh-vat droo-gee-ye oh-teh-lee?
Please clean my room.	Pozhaluysta, uberite v moyem nomere / Пожалуйста, уберите в моем номере	Poh-zhah-looy-stah, oo-bye-ree-tye v moh-yom noh-mye-reh
Could you please wake me at...?	Vi mozhete razbudit menya v...? / Вы можете разбудить меня в...?	Vee moh-zheh-tye raz-boo-deet meh-nya v...?
I would like to check out.	Ya hochu osvobodit nomer / Я хочу освободить номер	Ya hoh-choo os-voh-boh-deet noh-myer

Authorities

	Translation (Latin / Cyrillic)	How to say it
It was a misunderstanding.	Eto nedorazumenie / Это недоразумение	E-toh nye-doh-rah-zoo-mye-nee-ye
I haven't done anything wrong.	Ya ne sdelal nichevo plohovo / Я не сделал ничего плохого	Yah ne sdye-lal nee-cheh-voh ploh-hoh-voh
Am I under arrest?	Ya arestovan? / Я арестован?	Yah a-reh-stoh-van?
Where are you taking me?	Kuda vi menya vedete? / Куда вы меня ведете?	Koo-dah vee meh-nya vye-dyo-tye?
I want to talk to a lawyer.	Ya hochu pogovorit s advokatom / Я хочу поговорить с адвокатом	Yah hoh-choo poh-goh-voh-reet s ad-voh-kah-tom
I am an American / British / Australian / Canadian citizen.	Ya amerikanskiy / britanskiy / avstraliyskiy / kanadskiy grazhdanin / Я американский / британский / австралийский / канадский гражданин	Yah a-mye-ree-kan-skeey / bree-tan-skeey / av-strah-leey-skeey / kah-nad-skeey grazh-dah-neen
I want to talk to the American / British / Australian / Canadian embassy / consulate.	Ya hochu pogovorit s amerikanskim / britanskim / avstraliyskim / kanadskim poslom /	Yah hoh-choo poh-goh-voh-reet s a-mye-ree-kan-skeem / bree-tan-skeem / av-strah-leey-skeem /

	konsulom / Я хочу поговорить с американским / британским / австралийским / канадским послом / консулом	kah-nad-skeem pos-lom / kon-soo-lom
Can I just pay a fine now?	Ya mogu prosto oplatit shtraf? / Я могу просто оплатить штраф?	Yah moh-goo proh-stoh ohp-lah-teet shtrahf?

Bars, Restaurants and Food

	Translation (Latin / Cyrillic)	How to say it
I would like to make a reservation for tonight.	Ya hochu zakazat stolik na sevodnyashniy vecher / Я хочу заказать столик на сегодняшний вечер	Yah hoh-choo zah-kah-zat' stoh-leek nah sye-voh-dnya-shneey veh-chyer
I would like to make a reservation for tomorrow night.	Ya hochu zakazat stolik na zavtrashniy vecher / Я хочу заказать столик на завтрашний вечер	Yah hoh-choo zah-kah-zat' stoh-leek nah zah-ftrah-shneey veh-chyer
I have a reservation.	Ya zakazival stolik / Я заказывал столик	Ya zah-kah-zee-val stoh-leek
Can I have a table for two please?	Mne nuzhen stolik dlya dvoih, pozhaliysta / Мне нужен столик для двоих, пожалуйста	Mnye noo-zhen stoh-leek dlya dvoh-eeh, poh-zhah-looy-stah
When is closing time?	Vo skolko vi zakrivayetes? / Во сколько вы закрываетесь?	Voh skoh-lkoh vee zah-kree-vah-ye-tes'?
Do you know a good restaurant?	Vi mozhete posovetovat horoshiy restoran? / Вы можете посоветовать хороший ресторан?	Vee moh-zheh-tye poh-soh-vye-toh-vat' hoh-roh-sheey res-toh-ran?
Do you serve	Vi prodayete	Vee proh-dah-yo-tye

alcohol?	alkogolniye napitki? / Вы продаете алкогольные напитки?	al-koh-gol-nee-ye nah-peet-kee?
Can we please see the menu?	Mogu ya uvidet menyu? / Могу я увидеть меню?	Moh-goo yah oo-vyi-dyet' mye-nyoo?
Do you have a children's menu?	U vas est detskoye meyu? / У вас есть детское меню?	Oo vas yest' dyet-sko-ye mye-nyu?
What is today's special?	Kakoye sevodnya blyudo dnya? / Какое сегодня блюдо дня?	Kah-koh-je sye-voh-dnya blyu-doh dnya?
Is there a house specialty?	U vas est blyuda ot shef-povara? / У вас есть блюда от шеф-повара?	Oo vas yest blyu-dah ot shef-poh-vah-rah?
Is there a local specialty?	U vas est blyuda natsionalnoy kuhni? / У вас есть блюда национальной кухни?	Oo vas yest blyu-dah nah-tsee-oh-nal-noy kooh-nee?
What do you recommend?	Shto vi posovetuyete? / Что вы посоветуете?	Shtoh vee poh-soh-vye-too-ye-tye?
Can I look in the kitchen?	Ya mogu vzglyanut na kuhnyu? / Я могу взглянуть на кухню?	Yah moh-goo vzglya-noot' na kooh-nyu?
A la carte	A lya kart / А-ля карт	Ah-lya kart
Breakfast	Zavtrak / Завтрак	Zahv-trahk
Lunch	Lanch / Ланч	Lanch

Dinner	Obyed / Обед	Oh-byed
Supper	Uzhin / Ужин	Oo-zheen
Salt	Sol' / Соль	Sol'
Pepper	Perets / Перец	Pye-rets
Black pepper	Cherniy perets / Черный перец	Chyor-neey pye-rets
Butter	Maslo / Масло	Mas-loh
Cream	Slivki / Сливки	Sleev-kee
Chicken	Kuritsa / Курица	Koo-ree-tsah
Fish	Riba / Рыба	Ree-bah
Ham	Svinina / Свинина	Svee-nee-nah
Beef	Govyadina / Говядина	Goh-vya-dee-nah
Veal	Tyelyatina / Телятина	Tye-lya-tee-nah
Sausage	Sosiska / Сосиска	Soh-sees-kah
Eggs	Yaytsa / Яйца	Yay-tsah
Cheese	Sir / Сыр	Seer
Salad	Salat / Салат	Sah-lat
Vegetables	Ovoshchi / Овощи	Oh-voh-shchee
Fruit	Frukti / Фрукты	Frook-tee

Fresh	Svezhiy / Свежий	Svye-zheey
Toast	Tost / Тост	Tost
Bread	Hleb / Хлеб	Hlyeb
Sugar	Sahar / Сахар	Sah-har
Rice	Ris / Рис	Rees
Noodles	Vermishel' / Вермишель	Ver-mee-shel'
Pasta	Pasta / Паста	Pas-tah
Beans	Bobi / Бобы	Boh-bee
Tea	Chay / Чай	Chay
Coffee	Kofe / Кофе	Koh-fye
Milk	Moloko / Молоко	Mah-lah-koh
Juice	Sok / Сок	Sok
Orange juice	Apelsinoviy sok / Апельсиновый сок	Ah-pel-see-noh-veey sok
Lemon	Limon / Лимон	Lee-mon
Soft drink	Bezalkogolniye napitki / Безалкогольные напитки	Bez-al-koh-gol-nee-ye nah-peet-kee
Ice	Lyod / Лёд	Lyod

Coke	Kola / Кола	Koh-lah
Water	Voda / Вода	Voh-dah
Bubbly water	Gazirovannaya voda / Газированная вода	Gah-zee-roh-van-nah-yah voh-dah
Tonic water	Tonik / Тоник	Toh-neek
Beer	Pivo / Пиво	Pee-voh
Wine	Vino / Вино	Vee-noh
White wine	Byeloye vino / Белое вино	Bye-loh-ye vee-noh
Red wine	Krasnoye vino / Красное вино	Kras-noh-ye vee-noh
Whiskey	Viski / Виски	Vees-kee
Rum	Rom / Ром	Rom
Vodka	Vodka / Водка	Vot-kah
A bottle	Butilka / Бутылка	Boo-teel-kah
I am a vegetarian.	Ya vegetarianets / Я вегетарианец	Yah vye-ge-tah-ree-ah-nets
I don't eat meat.	Ya ne yem myaso / Я не ем мясо	Yah nye yem mya-soh
I don't eat pork.	Ya ne yem svininu / Я не ем свинину	Yah nye yem svee-nee-nuh

I want a dish containing...	Ya hochu blyudo s… / Я хочу блюдо с…	Yah hoh-choo blyu-doh s…
I only eat kosher food.	Ya yem tolko koshernuyu yedu / Я ем только кошерную еду	Yah yem tol-koh koh-sher-noo-yoo yeh-dooh
I'm allergic to...	U menya allergiya na… / У меня аллергия на…	Oo mye-nyah al-ler-gee-yah nah…
Waiter!	Ofitsiant! / Официант!	Oh-fee-tsee-ant!
Waitress!	Ofitsiantka! / Официантка!	Oh-fee-tsee-ant-kah!
Excuse me, waiter?	Izvinyite, ofitsiant? / Извините, официант?	Eez-vee-nyee-tye, oh-fee-tsee-ant!
Excuse me, waitress?	Izvinyite, ofitsiantka? / Извините, официантка?	Eez-vee-nyee-tye, oh-fee-tsee-ant-kah!
May I have a glass of...?	Hochu zakazat stakan… / Хочу заказать стакан…	Hoh-choo zah-kah-zat' stah-kan…
May I have a cup of...?	Hochu zakazat chashku… / Хочу заказать чашку…	Hoh-choo zah-kah-zat' chash-koo…
May I have a bottle of...?	Hochu zakazat butilku… / Хочу заказать бутылку…	Hoh-choo zah-kah-zat' boo-teel-koo…
Can I have a fork?	Mnye nuzhna vilka / Мне нужна вилка	Mnye noozh-nah veel-kah
Can I have a spoon?	Mnye nuzhna lozhka / Мне нужна ложка	Mnye noozh-nah lozh-kah

Can I have a knife?	Mnye nuzhen nozh / Мне нужен нож	Mnye noo-zhen nozh
Can I have a plate?	Mnye nuzhna tarelka / Мне нужна тарелка	Mnye noozh-nah tah-rel-kah
Can I have a glass?	Mnye nuzhen stakan / Мне нужен стакан	Mnye noo-zhen stah-kan
I am hungry.	Ya golodyen (golodnaya) / Я голоден (голодная)	Yah goh-loh-dyen (goh-loh-dnah-yah)
I am thirsty.	Ya hochu pit' / Я хочу пить	Yah hoh-choo peet'
I would like to order.	Ya hochu zakazat / Я хочу заказать	Yah hoh-choo zah-kah-zat'
I would like a water.	Ya hochu zakazat vodi / Я хочу заказать воды	Yah hoh-choo zah-kah-zat' voh-dee
I would like a coffee.	Ya hochu zakazat kofe / Я хочу заказать кофе	Yah hoh-choo zah-kah-zat' koh-fye
… with milk.	… s molokom / … с молоком	… s mah-lah-kom
I would like a tea.	Ya hochu zakazat chay / Я хочу заказать чай	Yah hoh-choo zah-kah-zat' chay
…. with lemon.	… s limomon / … с лимоном	… s lee-moh-nom
I would like an ice tea.	Ya hochu zakazat holodniy chay / Я хочу заказать холодный чай	Yah hoh-choo zah-kah-zat' hoh-lod-neey chay
I would like a soft	Ya hochu zakazat	Yah hoh-choo zah-

drink.	bezalkogolniy napitok / Я хочу заказать безалкогольный напиток	kah-zat' bez-al-koh-gol-neey nah-pee-tok
I would like a bottle of wine.	Ya hochu zakazat butilku vina / Я хочу заказать бутылку вина	Yah hoh-choo zah-kah-zat' boo-teel-koo vee-nah
Can you also bring us bread and butter?	Vi mozhetye prinesti nam hleb I maslo? / Вы можете принести нам хлеб и масло?	Vee moh-zhe-tye pree-nyes-tee nam hlyeb ee mas-loh?
What do you have for desserts?	Kakiye u vas yest desserti? / Какие у вас есть дессерты?	Kah-kee-ye oo vas yest dyes-syer-tee?
One more, please.	Eshchyo odin, pozhaluysta / Еще один, пожалуйста	Yesh-chyo oh-deen, poh-zhah-luy-stah
Another round, please.	Smena blyud, pozhaluysta / Смена блюд, пожалуйста	Smye-nah blyud
It was delicious.	Bilo ochen vkusno / Было очень вкусно	Bee-loh oh-chen' vkoos-noh
Please clear the plates.	Pozhaluysta, uberite posudu / Пожалуйста, уберите посуду	Poh-zhah-luy-stah, oo-bye-ryee-tye poh-soo-dooh
Where is the bathroom?	Gdye zdes tualet? / Где здесь туалет?	Gdye zdyes' too-ah-lyet?
Please bring me the bill.	Pozhaluysta, prinesite shchyot /	Poh-zhah-luy-stah, pree-nye-see-tye

	Пожалуйста, принесите счет	schyot

Colors and Numbers

	Translation (Latin / Cyrillic)	How to say it
White	Byeliy / Белый	Bye-leey
Yellow	Zholtiy / Желтый	Zhol-teey
Orange	Oranzheviy / Оранжевый	Oh-ran-zhe-veey
Red	Krasniy / Красный	Kras-neey
Green	Zelyoniy / Зеленый	Zye-lyo-neey
Brown	Korichneviy / Коричневый	Koh-reech-nye-veey
Blue	Siniy / Синий	See-neey
Purple	Sireneviy / Сиреневый	See-rye-nye-veey
Grey	Seriy / Серый	Sye-reey
Black	Chyorniy / Черный	Chyor-neey
Pink	Rozoviy / Розовый	Roh-zoh-veey
1.	odin / один	a-deen
2.	dva / два	dvah

3.	tri / три	tree
4.	chetirye / четыре	cheh-tee-ree
5.	pyat' / пять	pyat'
6.	shest' / шесть	shest'
7.	sem' / семь	syem'
8.	vosem' / восемь	voh-syem'
9.	dyevyat' / девять	dye-vyat'
10.	dyesyat' / десять	dye-syat'
11.	odinnatsat' / одиннадцать	a-deen-na-tsat'
12.	dvenatsat' / двенадцать	dvye-na-tsat'
13.	trinatsat' / тринадцать	tree-na-tsat'
14.	chetirnatsat' / четырнадцать	chye-teer-na-tsat'
15.	pyatnatsat' / пятнадцать	pyat-na-tsat'
16.	sheatnatsat' / шестнадцать	shest-na-tsat'
17.	semnatsat' / семнадцать	syem-na-tsat'
18.	vosemnatsat' / восемнадцать	voh-syem-na-tsat'
19.	dyevyatnatsat' / девятнадцать	dye-vyat-na-tsat'

20.	dvatsat' / двадцать	dvah-tsat'
21.	dvatsat' odin / двадцать один	dvah-tsat' a-deen
22.	dvatsat' dva / двадцать два	dvah-tsat' dvah
23.	dvatsat' tri / двадцать три	dvah-tsat' tree
24.	dvatsat' chetirye / двадцать четыре	dvah-tsat' cheh-tee-ree
25.	dvatsat' pyat' / двадцать пять	dvah-tsat' pyat'
26.	dvatsat' shest' / двадцать шесть	dvah-tsat' shest'
27.	dvatsat' sem' / двадцать семь	dvah-tsat' syem'
28.	dvatsat' vosem' / двадцать восесь	dvah-tsat' voh-syem'
29.	dvatsat' dyevyat' / двадцать девять	dvah-tsat' dye-vyat'
30.	tritsat' / тридцать	tree-tsat'
40.	sorok / сорок	soh-rok
50.	pyatdesyat / пятьдесят	pyat-dye-syat
60.	shestdyesyat / шестьдесят	shest-dye-syat
70.	semdesyat / семьдесят	syem-dye-syat
80.	vosemdesyat / восемьдесят	voh-syem-dye-syat

90.	dyevyanosto / девяносто	dye-vya-noh-stoh
100.	sto / сто	stoh
101.	sto odin / сто один	stoh a-deen
200.	dvyesti / двести	dvyes-tee
300.	trista / триста	trees-tah
400.	chetiresta / четыреста	chye-tee-ree-stah
500.	pyatsot / пятьсот	pyat-sot
600.	shestsot / шестьсот	shest-sot
700.	semsot / семьсот	syem-sot
800.	vosemsot / восемьсот	voh-syem-sot
900.	dyevyatsot / девятьсот	dye-vyat-sot
1000.	tisyacha / тысяча	tee-syah-chah
10,000	dyeasyat' tisyach / десять тысяч	dye-syat tee-syach
100,000	sto tisyach / сто тысяч	stoh tee-syach
1,000,000	million / миллион	meel-lee-on
Less.	Men'she / Меньше	Myen'-sheh
Half.	Polovina / Половина	Poh-loh-vee-nah

| More. | Bol'she / Больше | Bol'-sheh |

Directions and Transportation

	Translation (Latin / Cyrillic)	How to say it
North	Syever / Север	Sye-vyer
South	Yug / Юг	Yoog
West	Zapad / Запад	Zah-pad
East	Vostok / Восток	Voh-stok
Uphill	Vverh / Вверх	Vvyerh
Downhill	Vniz / Вниз	Vneez
Left	Levo / Лево	Lye-voh
Right	Pravo / Право	Prah-voh
Straight ahead.	Pryamo / Прямо	Prya-moh
To the left.	Nalevo / Налево	Nah-lye-voh
Turn left.	Povernite nalevo / Поверните налево	Po-vyer-nee-tye nah-lye-voh
To the right.	Napravo / Направо	Nah-prah-voh
Turn right.	Povernite napravo / Поверните направо	Po-vyer-nee-tye nah-prah-voh
How do I get to...?	Kak dobratsya do...? / Как добраться	Kak do-brah-tsah do...?

	до…?	
… the bus station?	… avtobusnoy ostanovki? / … автобусной остановки?	… av-toh-boos-noy os-tah-nov-kee?
… the airport?	… aeroporta? / … аэропорта?	… ah-eh-ro-por-tah?
… downtown?	… tsentra goroda? / … центра города?	…tsen-trah goh-roh-dah?
… the train station?	… vokzala? / … вокзала?	… vok-zah-lah?
… the youth hostel?	… studencheskovo hostela? / … студенческого хостела?	… stoo-dyen-ches-koh-voh hos-the-lah?
… the hotel?	… otelya? / … отеля?	… oh-the-lya?
… the embassy?	… posol'stva? / … посольства?	… poh-sol'-stvah?
… the consulate?	… konsul'stva? / … консульства?	… kon-sul'-stvah?
Where is the bus / train station?	Gdye nahoditsya avtobusnaya ostanovka / vokzal? / … Где находится автобусная остановка / вокзал?	Gdye nah-hoh-dee-tsah av-to-boos-nah-ya os-ta-nov-kah / vok-zal?
Excuse me, I am looking for the ticket office.	Izvinite, ya ishchu biletnuyu kassu / Извините, я ищу билетную кассу	Iz-vi-nyi-tye, yah ish-choo bee-lyet-noo-yoo kas-soo

I would like a one way ticket to....	Mne nuzhen odun bilet do... / Мне нужен один билет до...	Mnye noo-zhen a-deen bee-lyet do...
I would like a round trip ticket to....	Mne nuzhen bilet v obe storonu do... / Мне нужен билет в обе стороны до...	Mnye noo-zhen bee-lyet v oh-bye stoh-roh-nee
I would like to sit in the smoking car.	Mne nuzhen bilet v kuryashchem salone / Мне нужен билет в курящем салоне	Mnye noo-zhen bee-lyet v koo-ryash-chem sah-loh-nye
I would like to sit in the non-smoking car.	Mne nuzhen bilet v nekuryashchem salone / Мне нужен билет в некурящем салоне	Mnye noo-zhen bee-lyet v nye-koo-ryash-chem sah-loh-nye
Where does this train / bus go?	Vo skolko othodit avtobus / poezd? / Во сколько отходит автобус?	Vo skol'-koh ot-hoh-deet av-toh-boos / poh-yezd?
Where is the train / bus to...?	Kuda idet avtobus / poezd? / Куда идет автобус / поезд?	Koo-dah ee-dyet av-toh-boos / poh-yezd?
Does this train / bus stop in...?	Etot avtobus / poezd ostanavlivayetsya v...? / Этот автобус / поезд останавливается в...?	Eh-tot av-toh-boos / poh-yezd os-tah-nav-lee-vah-ye-tsah v...?
What is the departure and arrival time?	Kakoye vremya pribitiya I otpravki? / Какое время прибытия и отправки?	Kah-koh-ye vrye-myah pree-bee-tee-yah ee ot-prav-kee?

How much is a first class ticket?	Skolko stoit bilet v perviy klass? / Сколько стоит билет в первый класс?	Skol'-koh stoh-eet bee-lyet v pyer-veey klass?
Entrance.	Vhod / Вход	Vhod
Exit.	Vihod / Выход	Vee-hod
Where is the bus stop?	Gdye nahoditsya ostanovka avtobusa? / Где находится остановка автобуса?	Gdye nah-hoh-dee-tsah os-tah-nov-kah av-th-boo-sah?
One way ticket.	Bilet v odnu storonu / Билет в одну сторону	Bee-lyet v od-noo stoh-roh-noo
A round trip ticket.	Bilet v obe storoni / Билет в обе стороны	Bee-lyet v oh-bye stoh-roh-nee
Do you go to...	Vi yedete v… / Вы едете в…	Vee ye-dye-tye v…&
Do you have a schedule?	U vas yest raspisaniye? / У вас есть расписание?	Oo vas yest ras-pee-sah-nee-ye?
Which direction do I have to go?	V kakom napravlenii mne nuzhno idti? / В каком направлении мне нужно идти?	V kah-kom nah-prav-lye-nee-yee mnye noozh-noh eet-tee?
How often do the trains run?	Kak chasto hodit poezd? / Как часто ходит поезд?	Kak chas-toh hoh-deet poh-yezd?
How many stops are there?	Kak mnogo ostanovok po puti? / Как много остановок попути?	Kak mnoh-goh os-tah-noh-vok poh-poo-tee?
Please tell me when	Pozhaluysta, skazhete	Poh-zhah-looy-stah,

37

we get there?	mne, kogda mi doyedem? / Пожалуйста, скажете мне когда мы доедем?	skah-zhe-tye mnye, koh-gdah mee doh-ye-dyem?
How do I get there?	Kak mne tuda dobratsya? / Как мне туда добраться?	Kak mnye too-dah doh-brah-tsah?
Where is the closest metro station?	Gdye nahoditsya blizhayshaya stantsiya metro? / Где находится ближайшая станция метро?	Gdye nah-hoh-dee-tsah blee-zhay-shah-yah stan-tsee-ya meh-troh?
How much is the fare?	Skolko stoit proezd? / Сколько стоит проезд?	Skol'-koh stoh-eet proh-yezd?
How long does it stop?	Skolko dlitsya ostanovka? / Сколько длиться остановка?	Skol'-koh dlee-tsah os-tah-nov-kah?
From what platform does it leave?	S kakoy platformi on otpravlyayetsya? / С какой платформы он отправляется?	S kah-koy plat-for-mee on ot-prav-lya-ye-tsah?
Do I have to change trains?	Mne nuzhno budet peresazhivatsya na drugoy poezd? / Мне нужно будет пересаживаться на другой поезд?	Mnye nuzh-noh boo-dyet pye-rye-sah-zhee-vah-tsah nah droo-goy poh-ezd?
Is this place taken?	Eto mesto svobodno? / Это место свободно?	Eh-toh myes-toh svoh-bod-noh?
How much does it cost?	Skolko eto stoit? / Сколько это стоит?	Skol'-ko eh-toh stoh-

		eet?
Where do I get off?	Gdye mne vihodit'? / Где мне выходить?	Gdye mnye vee-hoh-deet'?
What time does the train leave?	Kogda otpravlyayetsya poezd? / Когда отправляется поезд?	Kog-dah ot-prav-lya-ye-tsah poh-ezd?
Towards the...	Po napravleniyu k... / По направлению к...	Poh nap-rav-lye-nee-yoo k...
Past the...	Mimo... / Мимо...	Meemoh...
Before the...	Pered... / Перед...	Pye-ryed...
Street	Ulitsa / Улица	Oo-lee-tsah
Intersection	Perekrestok / Перекресток	Pye-rye-kryos-tok
One way	Odnostoronneye dvizheniye / Одностороннее движение	Od-noh-storonyye dvee-zhye-nee-ye
No parking	Parkovka zapreshchena / Парковка запрещена	Par-kov-kah zah-presh-cheh-nah
Gas / petrol station	Avtozapravochnaya stantsiya / Автозаправочная станция	Av-to-zap-rah-voch-nah-yah stan-tsee-ya
Gas / petrol	Benzin / Бензин	Ben-zeen
Diesel	Dizel' / Дизель	Dee-zel'

Fare	Stoimost bileta / Стоимость билета	Stoh-ee-most bee-lye-tah
Speed limit	Predelnaya skorost' / Предельная скорость	Prye-dyel'-nah-yah skoh-rost'
Taxi!	Taksi! / Такси!	Ta-ksee!
Take me to...., please.	Otvezite menya k..., pozhaluysta / Отвезите меня к..., пожалуйста	Ot-vye-zee-tye mye-nya k..., poh-zhah-luy-stah
How much does it cost to go to...?	Skolko budet stoit' doehat' do...? / Сколько будет стоить доехать до...	Skol'-koh boo-dyet stoh-eet' doh-ye-hat' doh...?
Take me there, please.	Otvezite menya tuda, pozhaluysta / Отвезите меня туда, пожалуйста	Ot-vye-zee-tye mye-nya too-dah, poh-zhah-luy-stah
Is there a subway in this city?	V etom gorode yest metro? / В этом городе есть метро?	V eh-tom goh-rog-dye yest' mye-troh?
Where can I buy a ticket?	Gdye ya mogu kupit' bilet? / Где я могу купить билет?	Gdye yah moh-goo koo-peet' bee-lyet?
Do you have a map showing the subway stops?	U vas yest karta so stantsiyami metro? / У вас есть карта со станциями метро?	Oo vas yest' kar-tah soh stan-tsee-ya-mee myet-roh?
Can you show me on the map?	Vi mozhete pokazat' na karte? / Вы можете показать на карте?	Vee moh-zhye-tye poh-kah-zat' nah kar-tye?

Please take me to this address.	Pozhaluysta, otvedite menya po etomu adresu / Пожалуйста, отведите меня по этому адресу	Poh-zhah-luy-stah, ot-vye-dee-tye mye-nya poh eh-toh-moo ad-rye-soo
Is it far from here?	Eto daleko ot syuda? / Это далеко отсюда?	Eh-toh dah-lye-koh ot-syoo-dah?
I am lost.	Ya poteryalsya / Я потерялся	Yah poh-tye-ryal-syah
I want to rent a car.	Ya hochu arendovat' mashinu / Я хочу арендовать машину	Yah hoh-choo ah-ryen-doh-vat' mah-shee-noo

Emergencies and Problem Phrases

	Translation (Latin / Cyrillic)	How to say it
Help!	Pomogitye! / Помогите!	Poh-moh-gee-tye!
What is wrong?	Shto sluchilos? / Что случилось?	Shtoh sloo-chee-los'?
Leave me alone.	Ostav'tye menya v pokoye / Оставьте меня в покое	Os-tav'-tye mye-nya v poh-koh-ye
Don't touch me!	Nye trogaytye menya! / Не трогайте меня!	Nye troh-gay-tye mye-nya!
I will call the police.	Ya vizovu politsiyu / Я вызову полицию	Yah vee-zoh-voo poh-lee-tsee-too
Police!	Politsiya! / Полиция!	Poh-lee-tsee-yah!
Stop! Thief!	Lovitye! Vor! / Ловите! Вор!	Loh-vee-tye! Vor!
It's an emergency.	Eto srochno / Это срочно	Eh-toh sroh-chnoh
I need help.	Mnye nuzhna pomoshch / Мне нужна помощь	Mnye noozh-nah poh-poshch
I'm lost.	Ya poteryalsya / Я потерялся	Yah poh-tye-ryal-sya

Medical

	Translation (Latin / Cyrillic)	How to say it
I have pain.	Mnye bol'no / Мне больно	Mnye bol'-noh
I have a stomach ache.	U menya bolit zhivot / У меня болит живот	Oo mye-nya boh-leet zhee-vot
I am a diabetic.	Ya diabyetik / Я диабетик	Yah dee-ah-bye-teek
I have backache.	U menya bolit spina / У меня болит спина	Oo mye-nya boh-leet spee-nah
I have a toothache.	U menya bolit zub / У меня болит зуб	Oo mye-nya boh-leet zoob
I do not feel good.	Mnye nehorosho / Мне нехорошо	Mnye nye-hoh-roh-shoh
I have chest-pain.	U menya bolit v grudi / У меня болит в груди	Oo mye-nya boh-leet v groo-dee
I had a heart attack.	U menya serdyechniy pristup / У меня сердечный приступ	Oo mye-nya syer-dyech-neey pree-stoop
I have cramps.	U menya spazmi / У меня спазмы	Oo mye-nya spaz-mee
I have a sore throat.	U menya bolit gorlo / У меня болит горло	Oo mye-nya boh-leet gor-loh

I am allergic to…	U menya allergiya na… / У меня аллергия на…	Oo mye-nya al-lyer-gee-ya nah…
I need a doctor.	Mnye nuzhen doktor / Мне нужен доктор	Mnye noo-zhen dok-tor
I need a dentist.	Mnye nuzhen dantist / Мне нужен дантист	Mnye noo-zhen dan-teest
I need a nurse.	Mnye nuzhna medsestra / Мне нужна медсестра	Mnye noozh-nah myed-syes-trah
I feel sick.	Mnye ploho / Мне плохо	Mnye ploh-hoh
I have a headache.	U menya bolit golova / У меня болит голова	Oo mye-nya boh-leet goh-loh- vah
I think that I have the flu.	Mnye kazhetsya ya prostudilsya / Мне кажется я простудился	Mnye kah-zheh-tsah yah proh-stoo-deel-sya
I feel dizzy.	U menya kruzhitsya golova / У меня кружится голова	Oo mye-nya kroo-zhee-tsya goh-loh-vah
I feel nauseous.	Menya toshnit / Меня тошнит	Mye-nya tosh-neet
I have fever.	U menya grip / У меня грипп	Oo myenya greep
It hurts here.	Mnye bol'no zdyes / Мне больно здесь	Mnye bol'-noh zdyes'
Where's a hospital?	Gdye nahoditsya bol'nitsa? / Где находится	Gdye nah-hoh-dee-tsya bol'-nee-tsah?

	больница?	

Money

	Translation (Latin / Cyrillic)	How to say it
Do you accept American dollars?	Vi prinimayete amerikanskiye dollari? / Вы принимаете американские доллары?	Vee pree-nee-mah-ye-tye ah-mye-ree-kan-skee-yeh dol-lah-ree?
Do you accept Euros?	Vi prinimayete evro? / Вы принимаете евро?	Vee pree-nee-mah-ye-tye yev-roh?
Do you accept British pounds?	Vi prinimayete britanskiye funti? / Вы принимаете британские фунты?	Vee pree-nee-mah-ye-tye bree-tan-skee-ye foon-tee?
Do you accept credit cards?	Vi prinimayete kreditniye karti? / Вы принимаете кредитные карты?	Vee pree-nee-mah-ye-tye krye-deet-nee-yeh kar-tee&
Where can I find an ATM?	Gdye ya mogu nayti bankomat? / Где я могу найти банкомат?	Gdye yah moh-goo nay-tee ban-koh-mat?
Where can I withdraw money?	Gdye ya mogu snyat den'gi? / Где я могу снять деньги?	Gdye yah moh-goo snyat' den'-gee?
Where is the bank?	Gdye nahoditsya bank? / Где находится банк?	Gdye nah-hoh-dee-tsah bank?
What is the exchange rate?	Kakoy obmenniy kurs? / Какой	Kah-koy ob-myen-

	обменный курс?	neey koors?
Where can I get money changed?	Gdye ya mogu pomyenyat' den'gi? / Где я могу поменять деньги?	Gdye yah moh-goo poh-mye-nyat' den'-gee?
Can you change money for me?	Vi mozhetye pomenyat moi den'gi? / Вы можете поменять мои деньги?	Vee moh-zhe-tye poh-mye-nyat' moh-ee den'gee?
Where can I get a traveler's check changed?	Gdye ya mogu obnalichit' dorozhniye cheki? / Где я могу обналичить дорожные чеки?	Gdye yah moh-goo ob-nah-lee-cheet' doh-rozh-nee-ye chye-kee?
Can you change a traveler's check for me?	Vi mozhetye obnalichit' moi dorozhniye cheki? / Вы можете обналичить мои дорожные чеки?	Vee moh-zhe-tye ob-nah-lee-cheet' moh-ee doh-rozh-nee-ye chye-kee?

Shopping

	Translation (Latin / Cyrillic)	How to say it
I am looking for a shopping center.	Ya ishchu bolshoy magazin / Я ищу большой магазин	Yah eesh-choo bol-shoy mah-gah-zeen
Where can I find a department store?	Gdye ya mogu nayti univermag? / Где я могу найти универмаг?	Gdye yah moh-goo nay-tee oo-nee-ver-mag?
Where can I find a gift shop?	Gdye ya mogu nayti magazin podarkov? / Где я могу найти магазин подарков?	Gdye yah moh-goo nay-tee mah-gah-zeen poh-dar-kov?
Where can I find a market?	Gdye ya mogu nayti produktoviy magazin? / Где я могу найти продуктовый магазин?	Gdye yah moh-goo nay-tee proh-dook-toh-veey mah-gah-zeen?
Where can I find a clothing store?	Gdye ya mogu naytu magazin odyezhdi? / Где я могу найти магазин одежды?	Gdye yah moh-goo nay-tee mah-gah-zeen oh-dyezh-dee?
Please show me.	Pozhaluysta, pokazhite mnye / Пожалуйста, покажите мне	Poh-zhah-luy-stah, poh-kah-zhee-tye mnye
I'd like something.	Ya bi hotel shto-to / Я бы хотел что-то	Yah bee hoh-tyel shtoh-toh
I need...	Mnye nuzhno... /	Mnye noozh-noh...

	Мне нужно…	
… batteries	… batareyki / … батарейки	… bah-tah-rey-kee
… a pen	… ruchka / … ручка	… rooch-kah
… condoms	… prezervativi / … презервативы	… prye-zyer-vah-tee-vee
… change	… sdachu / … сдачу	… sdah-choo
… a postcard	… otkritku / … открытку	… ot-kree-tkoo
… postage stamps	… pochtoviye marki / … почтовые марки	… poch-toh-vee-yeh mar-kee
… a razor	… britvu / … бритву	… breet-voo
… shampoo	… shampun' / … шампунь	… sham-poon'
…aspirin	… aspirin / … аспирин	… as-pee-reen
… cold medicine	… lekarstva ot prostudi / … лекарства от простуды	… lye-kar-stva ot proh-stoo-dee
… stomach medicine	… lekarstva dlya zheludka / … лекарства для желудка	… lye-kar-stva dlya zheh-lood-kah
… soap	… milo / … мыло	… mee-loh
… tampons	… tamponi / … тампоны	… tam-poh-nee
… writing paper	… tualetnaya bumaga	… too-ah-lyet-nah-ya

	/ ... туалетная бумага	boo-mah-gah
... sunblock lotion	... krem ot zagara / ... крем от загара	... kryem ot zah-gah-rah
... toothpaste	... zubnaya pasta / ... зубная паста	... zoob-nah-yah pas-tah
... a toothbrush	... zubnaya shchyetka / ... зубная щетка	... zoob-nah-yah shchyot-kah
... an umbrella	... zontik / ... зонтик	... zon-teek
... English-language books	... knigi na angliyskom / ... книги на английском	... knee-gee na an-gleey-skom
... English-language magazines	... zhurnali na angliyskom / ... журналы на английском	... zhoor-nah-lee na an-gleey-skom
... English-language newspaper	... gazyeti na angliyskom / ... газеты на английском	... gah-zye-tee na an-gleey-skom
Do you take VISA?	Vi prinimayete Viza? / Вы принимаете Виза?	Vee pree-nee-mah-ye-tye Vi-zoo?
Do you take debit cards?	Vi prinimayete debetoviye karti? / Вы принимаете дебетовые карты?	Vee pree-nee-mah-ye-tye deh-bye-toh-vee-ye kar-tee?
Do you take American dollars?	Vi prinimayete amerikanskiye dollari? / Вы принимаете	Vee pree-nee-mah-ye-tye ah-mye-ree-kan-skee-ye dol-lah-ree?

	американские доллары?	
Do you have?	U vas yest? / У вас есть?	Oo vas yest'?
Do you have this in my size?	U vas yest eto moyevo razmera? / У вас есть моего размера?	Oo vas yest' eh-toh moh-ye-voh raz-mye-rah?
Expensive	Dorogo / Дорого	Doh-roh-goh
Cheap	Dyeshevo / Дешево	Dyo-sheh-voh
I'd like to try it on.	Ya hochu eto pomeryat' / Я хочу это померять	Yah hoh-choo eh-toh poh-mye-ryat'
It does not fit (me).	Mnye eto ne podhodit / Мне это не подходит	Mnye eh-toh nye pod-hoh-deet
It fits very well.	Mnye eto podhodit / Мне это подходит	Mnye eh-toh pod-hoh-deet
How much is it?	Skolko eto stoit? / Сколько это стоит	Skol'-koh eh-toh stoh-eet?
I can't afford it.	Ya ne mogu eto pozvolit' / Я не могу это позволить	Yah nye moh-goo eh-toh poz-voh-leet
That is too expensive.	Eto slishkom dorogo / Это слишком дорого	Eh-toh slish-kom doh-roh-goh
You're cheating me.	Vi menya obmanivayete / Вы меня обманываете	Vee ob-mah-nee-vah-ye-tye mye-nya
I'd like something else.	Mnye nuzhno shto-to drugoye / Мне	Mnye noozh-noh shtoh-toh droo-goh-

	нужно что-то другое	yee
I'm not interested.	Mnye eto ne nuzhno / Мне это не нужно	Mnye eh-toh nye noozh-noh
I don't want it.	Ya eto ne hochu / Я это не хочу	Yah eh-toh nye hoh-choo
I will take it.	Ya eto beru / Я это беру	Yah eh-toh bye-roo
Can I have a bag?	U vas yest sumka? / У вас есть сумка?	Oo vas yest soom-kah?
Can you ship it to my country?	Vi mozhetye dostavit' eto v moyu stranu? / Вы можете доставить это в мою страну?	Vee moh-zhe-tye dos-tah-veet' eh-toh v moh-yoo strah-noo?

Time and Date

	Translation (Latin / Cyrillic)	How to say it
Minute / Minutes	Minuta / Minuti / Минута / Минуты	Mee-noo-tah / Mee-noo-tee
Hour / Hours	Chas / Chasi / Час / Часы	Chas / Chah-see
Day / Days	Den' / Dni / День / Дни	Dyen' / Dnee
Week / Weeks	Nedelya / Nedeli / Неделя / Недели	Nye-dye-lya / Nye-dye-lee
Month / Months	Myesyats / Myesyatsi / Месяц / Месяцы	Mye-syats / Mye-sya-tsee
Year / Years	God / Goda / Год / Года	God / Goh-dah
3 o'clock AM	tri chasa utra / три часа утра	tree chah-sah oot-rah
8 o'clock AM	vosyem chasov utra / восем часов утра	voh-syem chah-sov oot-rah
2 o'clock PM	dva chasa dnya / два часа дня	dvah chah-sah dnyah
9 o'clock PM	dyevyat' chasov vechera / девять часов вечера	dye-vyat' chah-sov vye-chye-rah
Monday	Ponedelnik / Понедельник	Poh-nye-dyel-neek

English	Russian	Pronunciation
Tuesday	Vtornik / Вторник	Vtor-neek
Wednesday	Sreda / Среда	Srye-dah
Thursday	Chetverg / Четверг	Chet-vyerg
Friday	Pyatnitsa / Пятница	Pyat-nee-tsah
Saturday	Subbota / Суббота	Sub-boh-tah
Sunday	Voskresen'ye / Воскресенье	Vos-krye-syen'-ye
Today	Sevodnya / Сегодня	Seh-voh-dnya
Yesterday	Vchera / Вчера	Vcheh-rah
Tomorrow	Zavtra / Завтра	Zav-trah
This Week	Na etoy nedyele / На этой неделе	Nah eh-toy nye-dye-lye
Last Week	Na proshloy nedyele / На прошлой неделе	Nah prosh-loy nye-dye-lye
Next Week	Na sleduyushchey nedyele / На следующей неделе	Nah slye-doo-yoo-shchey nye-dye-lye
January	Yanvar' / Январь	Yan-var'
February	Fevral' / Февраль	Fev-ral'
March	Mart / Март	Mart

April	Aprel' / Апрель	Ap-ryel'
May	May / Май	Muy
June	Iyun' / Июнь	Ee-yoon'
July	Iyul' / Июль	Ee-yool'
August	Avgust / Август	Av-goost
September	Sentyabr' / Сентябрь	Syen-tyabr'
October	Oktyabr' / Октябрь	Ok-tyabr'
November	Noyabr' / Ноябрь	Noh-yabr'
December	Dekabr' / Декабрь	Dye-kabr'
June 13th, 2003	trinadtsatoye iyulya dve tishyachi tretyevo goda / тринадцатое июля две тысячи третьего года	tree-nah-tsah-toh-ye ee-yoo-lya dvye tee-sya-chee trye-tye-voh goh-dah
October 21st, 1999	dvadsat' pervoye oktyabrya tisyacha dyevyatsot devyanosto devyatovo goda / двадцать первое октября тысяча девятьсот девяносто девятого года	dva-tsat' pyer-voh-ye ok-tyab-rya tee-sya-chah dye-vya-tsot dye-vya-noh-sto dye-vya-toh-voh goh-dah

I sincerely hope you will get as much pleasure from this phrase book as I have had making it.

Now please go enjoy the beautiful country of Russia with your

newly learned language skills...

Printed in Great Britain
by Amazon